Danielle Bloom

Never Give up!! :)

ICEBOUND!

The Adventures of Young George Sheldon and the SS *Michigan*

Valerie van Heest

Ernest Shackleton *Photo courtesy of NOAA Image Library and enhanced by the author*

"Difficulties are just things to overcome, after all."
- Sir Ernest Shackleton

On August 1, 1914 Sir Ernest Shackleton set out from England on an expedition aboard the three-masted schooner *Endurance* in an attempt to be the first to cross Antarctica at the South Pole. Just when the ship had nearly reached land, the pack ice closed in, trapping the ship. The currents moved the ice pack and the *Endurance* northwest away from their destination. The crew stayed on their ship hoping the ice would set them free, but instead after ten months, the ice crushed their vessel and took it to the bottom of the sea.

Shackleton and his twenty-eight crew members took to the ice towing three small lifeboats. Despite the extreme cold and severe hardships, they managed to reach solid ground on the deserted Elephant Island on April 15, 1916. From there, Shackleton and five of his strongest men, set off in one of the lifeboats over open water to reach civilization on the southern coast of South Georgia Island. On August 30, 1916 he returned to Elephant Island, with the help of the Chilean Navy, to rescue all of his crew. Miraculously, everyone was still alive, however, they had suffered considerably during their four-month wait.

Although much is known about the famous voyage of *Endurance* that took place at the bottom of the earth, little is known about a similar epic journey that took place on Lake Michigan thirty years earlier when the world was still feeling the atmospheric effects of a volcanic eruption on the Indonesian island of Krakatoa. Three years after the eruption, those effects caused a severe winter storm which trapped a steamship and its crew of thirty on the frozen freshwater sea.

Read on...

Excitement

Clutching a brass oil lantern close to his husky body so the fierce wind wouldn't kill the flame, the young porter, George Sheldon, struggled up the steep steps to the wheelhouse of the steamship SS *Michigan*. In the lantern's glow, he saw snow swirling across the deck, spinning in the gusty wind that had churned ice-caked Lake Michigan into heaving swells. The steel steamer pounded as it broke into a solid field of pack ice like a battering ram. George wrapped his free arm around the railing to keep from falling. In the workroom near the stern he had filled all the ships' lanterns with oil and trimmed their wicks, and now he had to deliver this one to the wheelhouse to provide light for the long night ahead.

As George swung open the door, the wind slammed it against the wall, rattling the windows that surrounded the big ship's wheel. Startled, Captain Redmond Prindiville shouted from within his long, grey, wool coat and captain's hat.

"Get in here, boy, and close that door fast!"

As George struggled with the door, Captain Prindiville rubbed his hands quickly to warm them, then once again grabbed the wheel, nudging the ship through the ice against the wind.

George hung the lantern, then stared out the wheelhouse windows as the snow on his smooth, round face melted from the warmth of the room. The floating sea of ice loomed white against the dark water, then disappeared beyond the bow, like a ghost in the darkness. He could hardly believe that SS *Michigan* had left the port of Grand Haven, Michigan, early that morning when the sky was clear blue and not a breath of wind rippled the ice-caked water. The ship with its crew of thirty, rounded up after the winter lay-up, had steamed northwest all day on a special mission to rescue another steamship, *Oneida,* which had been trapped in the ice for three weeks.

Stuck twenty miles offshore, *Oneida's* passengers would never survive the hike over treacherous ice flows that could collapse and shift, knocking a person down or even swallowing him whole. The people, the ship and the 717 tons of flour in *Oneida's* cargo hold had to be saved. The mission had looked easy until the storm whipped up unexpectedly. Still, George knew if any ship could do it, SS *Michigan* could with Captain Prindiville at the helm!

4

"It looks like we have a long night ahead of us," the Captain said, releasing the wheel for another second to warm his hands. "Keep those lanterns burning bright. It's the only way folks on shore will know we are still making headway."

George nodded, doing his duty as the youngest crewman, but inside he was a bit worried. This was his first year serving on board a lake steamer and he was used to just handling the baggage and special requests from passengers during summer runs across the lake. "Do you think the ship will be able to get through the ice, sir?" He knew that the 212-foot-long SS *Michigan*, with steel cladding over its wooden hull, could plow through almost anything, but the ice on this crazy water seemed to want to climb up the sides and hold them fast.

The Captain glanced at George with a smile. "We'll cut through the ice like butter." His smile disappeared though, when his eyes returned to the snowy darkness where the wind was gathering strength. "I just wish," the Captain said almost to himself, "that the snow hadn't come so soon."

He sighed, then smiled again at George, a smile that George liked. The Captain had thirteen children and George enjoyed feeling as if the Captain considered him number fourteen. Having lost both of his parents a few years before, the only family George had was his older brother and his new sister-in-law, with whom he lived in Grand Haven.

"Finish passing out the lanterns, then turn in for the night," the Captain ordered. "Before you know it, we will be steaming back to Grand Haven with *Oneida* right behind us."

If the weather doesn't get any worse, George thought. With a quick nod and an "Aye, Cap'n," he left to carry out his orders.

Confinement

But the weather did get worse! As the pale grey morning dawned, George tossed and turned in his bunk. When he realized he didn't feel the usual rocking of the boat that meant they were steaming full speed ahead, he threw off his blanket and dropped his feet to the deck. That's when he noticed he was standing at an awkward angle. He hurried across the slanting deck to the porthole. No water. No sky. All he could see was a solid wall of white.

"I think we're trapped in the ice!" he called out to his bunkmates, but his announcement met with silence. The room was empty. As George hurriedly pulled on his boots, he wondered if the same thing happened to the *Michigan* that had happened to the *Oneida*. He knew that three weeks ago, when the temperature had dropped and the wind shifted, it pushed the ice chunks together like pieces of a puzzle, locking *Oneida* in solid ice far off shore. They were on a mission to break through the ice to free *Oneida*. *Now who would come to their rescue?*, he worried.

George wanted answers. Grabbing his overcoat, he rushed out of the crews' quarters, ran past the galley, forward through the chain locker where the windlass that raised and lowered the anchors was located, up the narrow stairway and up yet another set of stairs on the port side to the wheelhouse to see the Captain. Instead, he found First Mate, Joseph Russell. "What's going on?" George asked, out of breath.

"The Captain is out on the ice with some of the mates trying to chop us free."

"So it's true," George muttered.

Joseph led him outside to the starboard deck and pointed down over the rail to the men wielding axes and picks. "Looks like the ice is pretty solid already!"

Through the grey of morning, George could see they were working hard to try to free the hull from the grip of the ice, but it looked rather hopeless.

It must be strange to stand on solid ground, where yesterday there was only water, George thought.

Within an hour, Captain Prindiville returned to the wheelhouse. "The ice is solid. Nearly two feet thick. We're not going anywhere." He told Joseph to inform the rest of the crew to keep the steam up in the boilers and go about their regular duties until the ice loosened up.

As George left the wheelhouse he wondered, *Does anyone on shore even know we're trapped?*

8

Worry

The ice did not let go of its grip on the *Michigan*. In the week since becoming trapped, George busied himself with shipboard chores. The temperature dropped to 18 degrees below zero and the blizzard buried the ship in two feet of snow. While the engineer worked to keep the boilers filled with coal to generate steam and heat the ship, George kept the lanterns filled with oil. If a rescue ship was on the way, the black cloud of smoke billowing from the smokestack would guide them by day and the lantern light would guide them at night.

Besides chores, there was not much to do and George was bored. Meals were all he had to look forward to. Every day the crew would gather in the galley, across from the bunk room, where George and nine other crewmen slept. It was warmest there, where the cook, Charles Robinson, served up beef stew and biscuits, making do with the supplies they had on board. They passed the time telling jokes, singing songs, and playing cards.

As Charlie prepared Saturday night's dinner, George noticed the Captain interrupt his work to take the cook aside. He couldn't hear what the two men were whispering, but soon after, the Captain called for everyone's attention.

"Looks like we're running low on food and there seems to be no break in the weather. I've told Mr. Robinson to start rationing. Only one meal per day. Eat up tonight. I'm sorry boys, there will be nothing else until tomorrow night." George looked around the cabin. No one said a word as Charlie started dishing up the stew.

Despite a filling dinner, George awoke Sunday morning to a growling stomach. How would he ever last until dinner with nothing to eat? In the quiet of morning, something else was making noise too. He could hear creaking coming from the cargo hold one deck below his quarters. Each time the noise started, the ship seemed to quiver and tremble. The ice must be pressing in on all sides. Just the day before, George had heard First Mate Russell tell a story of another ship crushed by the ice a few years ago. It sank. None of the crew had survived.

Eagerness

On the morning of the ninth day since they set out, Captain Prindiville came down to the crews' quarters early. "Wake up! Wake up, boys! I've got some important news to tell you." Startled out of a deep sleep, George tumbled down from his bunk to join the men gathering across the corridor in the galley. *Maybe it's good news,* he hoped.

"It stopped snowing some time last night, boys, but there's no sign of open water. By my reckoning, the ice has been moving us south quite a ways, but it doesn't look like it will break up any time soon."

George's short-lived hope was dashed.

Turning to First Mate Russell, the Captain gave orders. "Joseph, I want you to take sixteen men and enough warm clothes and supplies and try to make it back to Grand Haven for help. There's just not enough food for everyone. The rest of us will stay on board and try to get the ship safely home." George knew it would take at least a dozen men to sail the ship back to Grand Haven if the ice loosened its grip.

As Joseph started selecting his crew, George wondered if he would be picked. Walking on the ice would be dangerous. What if it were thin and he fell through? The cold water would kill him in minutes. But if he stayed on board the ship, he would go hungry. Or worse yet, he could die if the ship sank. At least if he went along, he would be doing something. He hated having nothing to do. Just before Joseph picked the last man, George piped up. "Can I go along?"

Captain Prindiville turned with a concerned look in his eyes. Slowly, a hint of that smile George loved to see formed on his face. "You go, George…just be careful on that ice. Get home to your brother safely."

George gathered a few of his belongings but, before he joined the crew, he made sure the lanterns were filled and ready for his shipmates.

12

An hour later, carrying axes, ropes, rations, and blankets, George set out with First Mate Russell and fifteen other crewmen. The temperature was ten degrees below zero, and despite a clear day, the wind sounded like howling dogs. It scooped up the snow and pelted it against their exposed cheeks. It felt as though pins and needles were being thrown at George.

With nothing but a compass to lead them in the direction of the land they could not see, they trudged for the better part of the day through deep snow. Sometimes they had to climb over six or eight-foot-high pressure ridges, where the ice had cracked and the two halves had risen up and frozen solid. It was tough going, but George was happy to be moving after more than a week being stuck on the ship. In the distance, the crashing and rumbling ice sounded like thunder. Even though the ice felt solid, George knew it was just like a huge raft moving over the open water. He watched for spots that could be thin because, if he plunged through, he knew the ice cold water would take his breath away, and his heavy clothes would pull him down below the ice.

It was mid afternoon when the ship's purser, William Kenny, who was walking just behind George, fell down with a scream. George turned back to help him and realized William had stepped on a thin spot where a crack was forming and broken through up to his right knee. He called to Joseph and within seconds they pulled him out. William's leg was soaking wet and it quickly froze when exposed to the frigid air. He lay on the ice grasping his leg and grimacing in pain. Joseph and George helped him to stand, but he collapsed. "I can't make it. Go on without me."

Knowing he would freeze to death if left there, George and Joseph supported him as they struggled over the patch of rough ice and continued eastward for the rest of the day through the coldest winter weather in decades. With no land in sight, George wondered if they would make it.

Relief

George, Joseph and William trudged along through the late afternoon following behind the other men. William fell several more times complaining he could barely feel his leg. Each time, they stopped and rested for a few minutes.

Finally, late in the day, George saw a long-hoped-for sight. "Land! I see land!" The men whooped and hollered, steam from their breaths clouding the air.

They struggled onward until day's end before the exhausted party finally reached shore. The half-frozen crew faced one last challenge before they could rest. The only way to possibly reach a cottage or farm for food and shelter would be to climb the steep bluff. After the dangerous and difficult hike across the ice with his empty stomach growling with every step, the bluff looked like a mountain to George.

Using his last bit of strength, George struggled up the nearly vertical incline, using the roots and branches to help pull him up, but his hands were so cold that he kept loosing his grip and slipping backward. Finally, he clawed his way over the edge. In the distance he could see a farmhouse and smoke was coming from the chimney. "There's a house!" he excitedly pointed.

George stumbled across the open field with the other men, on feet so cold he could barely feel them. Joseph arrived first and rapped on the door.

With a candlestick in one hand, a man cracked open the door a few inches. He looked surprised. George realized how strange they must look: seventeen shivering people wrapped in blankets huddled together on the porch. Joseph quickly offered an explanation, pointing out towards the frozen lake. "We are the crew of the SS *Michigan*. Our ship is trapped and we walked here across the ice."

The man thrust open the door. "Come in, get out of the cold, boys. I'm Levi Thomas. You're welcome to stay here with my family tonight."

"Where are we?" George asked as he passed into the comforting warmth of the house.

"Why you're in West Casco Township, young man." *My goodness*, George thought, *that is more than thirty miles south of Grand Haven. The ice sure moved the ship a long way.*

After the initial pain of thawing his fingers and toes, George sat by the fire and told Mr. Thomas the story about their week-long ordeal.

What a story it was!

Bravery

Despite sleeping in the first warm bed in more than a week, George tossed and turned all night, worried about Captain Prindiville and the remaining men on the ship. He thought about how hungry and miserable they must be. By the early morning he had a plan.

Mrs. Thomas was already preparing a big pot of oatmeal when George entered the kitchen. "I've made this for you, young man," she said as she handed him a mug of hot cocoa.

He sipped the sweet, warm drink as he listened to Joseph, who had apparently gotten up even earlier, talk to Levi about their need to find a tugboat capable of breaking through the ice to the SS *Michigan*. Levi suggested they try to catch the afternoon train at the Bravo station. It would take them north to Grand Haven where they could make those arrangements. He asked his two oldest sons to harness up the horses and take the crew inland to Bravo. After so many days of snowfall, it would be nearly impossible to make the journey on foot.

Fearing Joseph would not allow him to carry out the plan he had come up with overnight, George simply said he was too exhausted to go. "I'm not going to force

18

you, boy, but we're leaving soon as we finish up this oatmeal," Joseph told him.

As George and Levi watched the team of horses trudge off through the clearing, George revealed his true plan to Levi.

"Young man, you've got a lot of spunk to want to do this. When my boys get back with the horses, we'll go into town and get the things your Captain needs."

George was glad for the chance to help. He was a porter after all, and that meant it was his job to carry, move, and unload things. Of course, that was expected of him when the ship was carrying passengers during the summertime, but *why not when his own shipmates needed him most*, he thought.

19

Accomplishment

It had been four days since George had left for shore and he was sure that back in the wheelhouse of the SS *Michigan*, Captain Prindiville was keeping a close watch on the ice for any sign of open patches. The sky was clear that morning and the sun warmed George's back as he trudged along through the deep snow, pulling a sled behind him. He followed the plume of smoke on the horizon, but once he was a few miles off shore, he could see the silhouette of the ship. He figured it was now at least 20 miles from shore. *Maybe Captain Prindiville can see me through his spyglass*, he thought. He hoped that the Captain would not be too mad, especially when he learned everyone was safe.

The ship appeared larger and larger as George got nearer and, by late afternoon, after the sun had set and George was starting to get very cold, he saw some figures gathered on deck, waving. Then he heard a bell ring out. *It must be the Captain summoning the rest of the crew,* he figured.

Captain Prindiville met him down on the ice with questions. "Why are you back here? Is everyone all right?"

"I knew you would be hungry and bored, so I brought you these supplies," he replied, pointing at the sled. "The others took the train north to Grand Haven, to arrange for a rescue ship."

The Captain acted angry that George had disobeyed him, but the bear hug he gave George assured him the Captain was glad to see him. They climbed up through the cargo hold door and headed forward to the galley where the men were gathered to stay warm. George unloaded some slabs of meat, bags of flour, newspapers, tobacco and even some boxes of chocolates. For a crew who had been trapped in the ice for almost two weeks, George knew this was like Christmas morning!

20

"Without these supplies, we would have been forced to abandon ship tomorrow, something the owners would not be happy about. At least now there is a chance that we can hold out until help arrives," the Captain told George.

After the crew had their most satisfying dinner in a week, Captain Prindiville urged George to turn in early. "Aye, Aye, Captain, after I fill the oil lanterns. If a ship is on its way, they'll need the light to guide them."

As George settled into the snug sleeping bag on his bunk, the ship lurched. It was then he realized the grinding sound coming from the hull was worse than when he left. Before he faded into a deep sleep, his last thought was *Will the SS* Michigan *hold out until help arrives?*

Loneliness

By Monday, the sun shone brightly, but the lake was still frozen solid. In the two days since George returned, there was no sign of a rescue ship and no sign the ice was breaking up. George had come up with another plan. He climbed the stairs to the wheelhouse to see the Captain. "I've been thinking, sir. I would like to go back to shore to get enough supplies to wait out the winter."

"You go ahead home, son, but don't come back this time. We'll be OK."

That was at least half the permission George needed to set his plan in action. If he could get someone on shore to help him, they could gather enough supplies to get by for another month. Maybe then Captain Prindiville could save his ship.

The bright sun reflected off the snow as George began his journey, following the tracks he had made two days earlier on his trek out to the ship. It was so quiet, the only sound he could hear was the squeak of his boots on the crusty snow. The stillness made him feel very alone. He was so intent on getting to the ship the last time that he didn't realize how dangerous it was alone

on the ice. What if he fell in, like William? Who would help him? He would have to be extra cautious.

Having already made the hike across the ice twice, George had become good at picking the safest, most direct route to avoid difficult and dangerous terrain, but the ever-changing ice made for some complications. Within sight of shore, he tumbled down an ice ridge and lay stunned for a few minutes before he realized what had happened. He picked himself up and stumbled onward. It seemed that the ice nearest shore was the most treacherous since the water was shallower there and the wave action froze the surface unevenly.

It took George only about six hours to reach land this time and he realized that the ice must have moved the ship closer to shore. It was the familiar smoke from the Thomas' chimney that led George to the warmth that awaited him at the farm. Levi Thomas welcomed him back and George explained his new plan.

22

23

Happiness

After two days, George was ready to return to his ship. Levi Thomas had rallied six local men from Casco who agreed to help transport the supplies out to the stranded ship. With knapsacks and a sled packed with supplies, George blazed a trail for the team towards the ship. Again he headed towards the billowing black steam, but realized it was much farther north than the last trip.

"The ice must be drifting faster now," he told the other men. The trek would be longer than he figured and George knew it would be late afternoon by the time they reached the ship. It didn't snow that day and the wind was not too strong, which made the long hike to the ship tolerable.

This time when George arrived, Captain Prindiville just shook his head and smiled. George was happy he did not get mad at him for disobeying *half* his order.

The Casco men planned to return the next day, but overnight, another blizzard blew in, making it too dangerous to leave the ship. They, too, had become icebound!

24

Optimism

Two days later, George awoke at dawn. The blizzard had finally let up and, from his porthole, he could see patches of blue water in the distance. *The shift in wind must be breaking up the ice,* he hoped. He went to find Captain Prindiville to see what he thought.

"The ice seems pretty solid from here to shore, but it might not be too long before we can break ourselves free," the Captain told him. "With the supplies you brought out here, we should be able to make it for awhile, but let's send your Casco friends back home, now that the weather has let up." He suggested George remain behind with the crew this time.

Captain Prindiville ordered the lifeboat launched for the Casco men. Although a heavy burden to drag over the frozen lake, the lifeboat was insurance the men would need in case they encountered open water on their way home across the now churning ice pack.

Hours after the Casco men left, a stiff wind blew in from the south and the snow returned. The pack ice began closing in. George's hopes were again dashed. The ice would not set the ship free anytime soon.

25

Anxiety

Nearly three weeks had passed since the Casco men left for shore, and SS *Michigan* was still trapped. George had watched Captain Prindiville track the ship's movement as the ice pushed it steadily back towards the north until it was off shore from the small town of Holland. In those weeks the coal had been used up, and the ship was frigid. The food was almost gone too, and there was only enough oil to fill the lanterns one last night. The men had not had a bath for over a month and they smelled horrible. Their clothes were greasy and worn, and their hands and faces were red and raw from exposure to the cold. George felt miserable and he knew his shipmates did too.

Two days earlier George had gone down to the lower cargo deck and noticed a trickle of water coming into the ship where the ice had damaged the wooden hull despite its iron sheathing. He overheard the Captain and the engineer talking. They said it was only a matter of time before the ice would crush the hull and water would come rushing in, dragging the ship down.

The previous night and all through the morning, he heard creaks and groans as the ice tightened its grip. After 39 days fighting to save the ship, it appeared they might lose it.

26

Hope

The door to the wheelhouse flew open as George hurried in to see Captain Prindiville. "I just saw something out on the ice. I think it's a tugboat sent out to rescue us!"

"You're right, George," the Captain confirmed, handing George his spyglass so he could get a closer look. "It's the *Arctic*, but now it's icebound too. I saw it cutting through the ice towards us late last night. Good thing you kept the lanterns lit so the *Arctic's* crew could see us. They may be our only hope now."

"But how, if they're trapped, too?"

Just as George asked that question, the ship lurched violently, and he stumbled and had to brace himself against the ship's wheel. They could hear the ship groan louder than ever before. This was the moment George hoped would never happen.

"The ship's going down, isn't it, Captain?

"I'm afraid so," he stammered as he grabbed his spyglass, a chart, and threw two blankets over his shoulder. "It sounds like the hull has buckled. It's time to abandon ship and try to reach the tugboat."

27

Word spread fast among the crew and they gathered on the sloping deck with the few things they could carry. "Hurry up, everyone, abandon ship now! We don't have a minute to spare!" Captain Prindiville called out to his men. There was no time to launch the remaining lifeboat when the Captain ordered them off. Altogether, they moved quickly toward the tugboat several miles distant, hoping they would make it before the sun was gone.

Barely a quarter of a mile from the ship, George turned when he heard a loud rumbling and screeching noise. The ice began to open up like the jaws of a giant monster. Everyone watched in horror as the bow of the ship rose up. George could feel the frozen lake shake beneath his feet as the ship twisted and squirmed before being swallowed by the ice and slipping into the watery depths below. Captain Prindiville checked his pocket watch. It was 4:00 PM. "She's gone," he sadly announced. George turned so the other men would not see his tears.

Safety

After watching their ship disappear beneath the ice, the crew had to slow their pace and step carefully because the ice was beginning to break up. George realized that if the *Arctic* had not been within just a few miles of the SS *Michigan*, no one would have made it back to shore alive. He also knew that watching his ship sink was the hardest thing that Captain Prindiville had ever done.

The tugboat's crew welcomed the shipwreck survivors aboard just before night descended. Captain Prindiville, George, and the others spent the next few days icebound with the tugboat's crew. George hoped that the ice would melt and allow the tugboat to steam back to shore, but that was not to be.

After two days of waiting with nothing to do and little food, George was starving. He heard the tugboat crew talking about how little food they had left, so it was no surprise when Captain Prindiville made another announcement.

"Men, it is time for us to try for shore. George has crossed the ice four times now and with his guidance, I think we can make it."

Proud that the Captain recognized his skills, George was still worried. The last time he crossed the ice, he was well fed and rested. After more than a month of inactivity, little food, and extreme cold, this would be the most difficult ordeal he and the others would face. Now with the ice moving and without a lifeboat for backup, it would be more dangerous than ever. *I hope we can make it*, George thought.

30

Jubilation

On Monday, March 23, 1885, bundled in woolen blankets, Captain Prindiville and the last remaining men again took to the ice and headed east toward the far-off shore. George led the tired, haggard team carefully avoiding the thin patches and skirting around the pressure ridges. He knew that one wrong step might result in his death or the death of his friends.

Those last few miles were the toughest for George and the crew of SS *Michigan*. Exhausted, the ship's cook, Charles Robinson, gave up during the perilous journey. Captain Prindiville insisted he keep moving and he and George helped support him. George added Charles' pack to his own burden.

The ice was the roughest as they neared shore. There were deep fissures in the ice and many places where water formed in dangerous pools on the surface. George's legs ached, his feet were thoroughly wet and the throbbing made each step an effort. They struggled in single file following in George's well-placed footsteps.

When George's feet no longer bogged down in wet snow, he realized he had reached the beach. "Just a little farther," he hollered encouragingly to those behind him.

One by one the men gathered around George until all twelve men were huddled together, standing on solid land for the first time after 43 days of being icebound on Lake Michigan.

Despite the crew's obvious exhaustion, every man found the strength to pat George on the back. Captain Prindiville spoke what each must have been thinking, "Thanks to you, young man, we're all safe!"

But not the crew on the Arctic, thought George as he stomped his aching feet. *What about them?*

32

Epilogue

The crew of SS *Michigan* reached land several miles north of Holland, Michigan. They followed the shoreline south to the tall, white lighthouse that marked the entrance to Black Lake (today's Lake Macatawa), where they spent the night with the light keeper. The next morning they hiked seven miles inland through forested land to the train station in Holland where they caught the train back home to Grand Haven.

Arctic remained trapped for more than a week. Captain Kirby, owner of the tugboat, sent a relief party out to the tug with 150 pounds of flour, pork and other supplies. Escorting this relief party was none other than young George Sheldon. In April, the ice began breaking up and, *Arctic* and its crew steamed home safely.

Ironically, *Oneida,* the ship that SS *Michigan* had set out to rescue, had actually worked herself out of the ice on February 9th, the first day of *SS Michigan's* long ordeal. The rescuer had become the victim! But thanks to the dedication of young George Sheldon, all thirty men lived to tell their incredible story of patience, stamina, and heroism while icebound on Lake Michigan!

Wreck Hunters

Dedicated to preserving maritime history, scuba divers of Michigan Shipwreck Research Associates, (pictured clockwise, at right) Craig Rich, Ross Richardson, Valerie van Heest, Jack van Heest and Jan Miller set out to find the long lost wreck *Michigan*. They meticulously researched the sinking by collecting newspaper articles from February and March 1885 written about the ordeal that was then taking place on the lake. Hunting for clues the way detectives would, MSRA found three important pieces of information to help them create a probable search area in which to locate the sunken steamer:

1. The crew walked all day from *Arctic* and reached shore seven miles north of Holland.
2. *Arctic* was between two and six miles north and east of SS *Michigan* when it sank.
3. *Arctic* steamed southwest out of Grand Haven towards the trapped SS *Michigan*.

MSRA regularly partners with side scan sonar operator, David Trotter, who is responsible for locating over eighty Great Lakes' shipwrecks. Together they had located the wreck of the cargo steamer *H.C. Akeley* in 2001, and had the determination, experience and skills to find SS *Michigan*.

34

MSRA team *Photo by Catherine Rich*

David Trotter *Photo by author*

Side Scan Sonar

Sonar is a system that uses a torpedo-like device called a "fish" that is towed behind the research vessel. While running lanes in a pattern like mowing a lawn, the *fish* sends acoustical signals out on both sides and converts the return echoes into an image of the lake bottom, which is plotted on the topside chart recorder. Sonar can locate anything of mass that sits on the bottom, and it can also find unusual geological features. It takes an expert, like David Trotter, to interpret the images to determine whether or not they represent a sunken ship.

Side scan diagram Graphic by author

The Search

The team divided the probable search area into smaller sections numbered 1 through 13, in the order of highest probability. (See diagram at far right.)

During the 2003 expedition, MSRA covered section one and found nothing. During the 2004 expedition they covered section two and found a shipwreck about the same length as SS *Michigan*. Dives on the wreck revealed a 195-foot, steel, work barge, probably scuttled because it was too old to be useful. SS *Michigan* was still missing.

During the 2005 expedition, the team covered sections 3, 4, 5, 6 and 7 in six days and found nothing. On the last day of their expedition, MSRA discovered a target in 275 feet of water in section eight.

The image most definitely represented a shipwreck. It was just over 210 feet long. The dark area on the plot indicated a vessel of iron construction and the white area indicated that it sits upright on the bottom. Although everything matched what was known about SS *Michigan*, the team could not be sure of the shipwreck's identity until divers could visit the site and bring back photographs of the wreck. Recreational scuba divers normally limit their depth to 130' and this wreck was more than twice that deep. A specialized dive team would be needed.

36

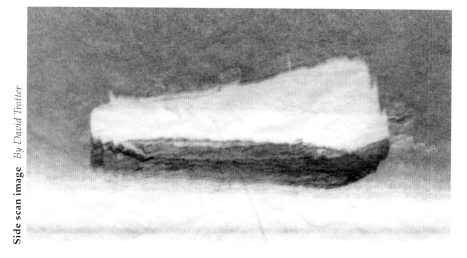

Side scan image *By David Trotter*

David Trotter and author on research vessel *Photo by Jack van Heest*

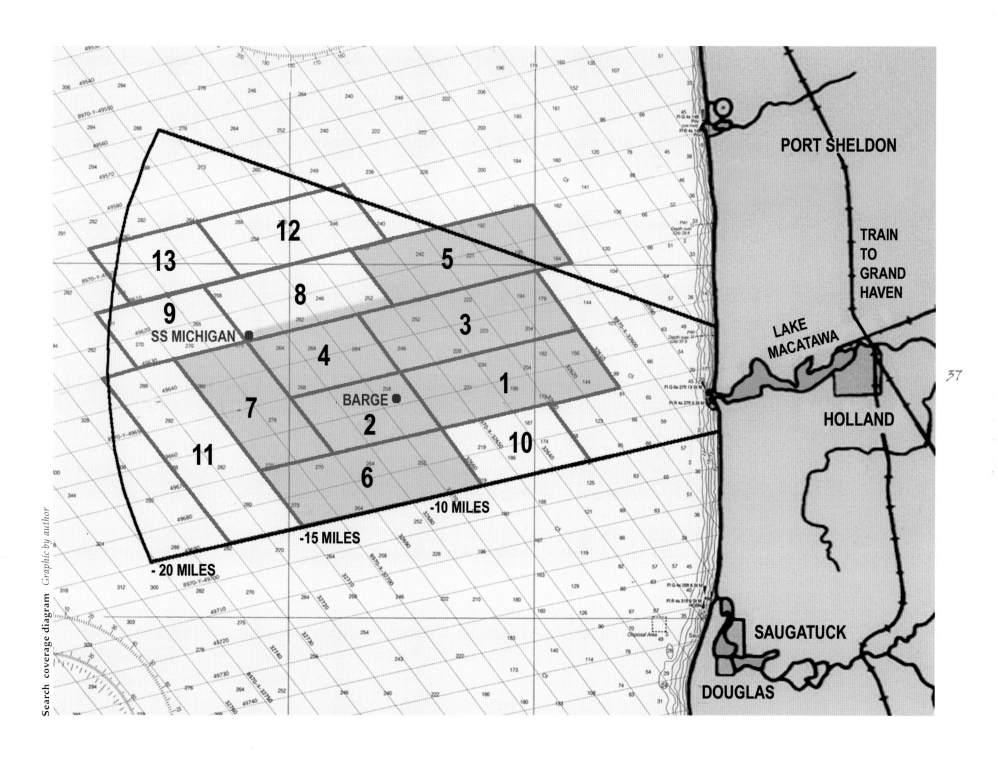

Search coverage diagram *Graphic by author*

PORT SHELDON

TRAIN
TO
GRAND
HAVEN

LAKE
MACATAWA

HOLLAND

SAUGATUCK

DOUGLAS

12

13

5

8

9

SS MICHIGAN

3

4

1

7

BARGE

2

11

10

6

-10 MILES

-15 MILES

- 20 MILES

37

The Dive

MSRA's technical dive team, Bob Underhill, Jeff Vos and Todd White, had the specialized training, equipment, and expertise to make this dangerous dive. In addition, they were skilled at using video and still cameras underwater.

They wore watertight *"drysuits"* with thick, long underwear to keep them warm in the year-round, 35-degree temperature at the bottom. To have enough air, they wore double tanks and carried two additional air cylinders filled with a special blend of air called *"tri-mix,"* which reduces the narcotic effects of nitrogen and the toxic effects of oxygen breathed under pressure. They could spend only 20 minutes on the wreck and would need to spend 45 minutes on their way up doing *"decompression,"* a slow process required to rid their bodies of excess nitrogen buildup in their body tissues.

With cameras in rigid acrylic housings, and lights to penetrate the darkness, the divers descended to the wreck. What they saw in the first few minutes convinced them that the team had found the final resting place of SS *Michigan*. The wreck is a time capsule revealing the ordeal the crew went through during their long days icebound on Lake Michigan.

38

Jeff Vos pauses near the port anchor at the bow   Photo by Robert Underhill

The Wreck

The shipwreck rests upright on the flat, sandy bottom. The wheelhouse, passenger cabins, and smokestack have all collapsed probably due to a hard impact with the bottom. Captain Prindiville's wheel, however, lies exposed and unhurt among the debris.

Artist's rendering of the wreck   *Drawing by Robert Doornbos*

The ship has sunk into the soft sand bottom up to its waterline, and so conceals the damage the ice must have done to the lower hull causing water to rush in. The forward mast and last remaining lifeboat lie fallen next to the hull. In position as they would have been while the ship was icebound, the anchors are secured at the bow. Just aft of the two anchors, the capstan, a round winching device used to raise the anchors, bears conclusive proof of the ship's identity: the name *Michigan* is engraved on its cover.

Zebra Mussels

The shipwreck SS *Michigan* is covered with many layers of zebra mussels. These small, fingernail-sized mollusks are native to freshwater lakes of southeast Russia. It is believed they were accidentally introduced into the lakes in 1988 from the ballast water of ocean-going ships that traveled from Russia through the St. Lawrence Seaway. Zebra mussels get their name from the striped pattern on their shells, though not all shells bear this pattern.

Zebra mussels are filter-feeding organisms. They remove particles from the water column as their food source, increasing water clarity and reducing pollution. Clearer water also has allowed the sunlight to penetrate deeper. For divers this means that their visibility underwater has much improved. In the early 1980s, Lake Michigan became pitch black at about 100 feet deep and even with an underwater light, divers could only see a few feet in front of them. Now, two decades after the mussels began filtering the water, divers on the wreck of SS *Michigan* are often able to see as far as 75 feet without the aid of artificial light.

In exchange for improved visibility, divers must contend with the presence of zebra mussels on shipwrecks. They attach to most anything using their string-like byssal threads which make it very hard to remove the mussels. Now shipwrecks, even those as deep as SS *Michigan*, are almost completely covered by the mussels. In order to see the name of the ship engraved on the capstan of SS *Michigan*, divers had to first scrape the mussels off.

Close-up view of a zebra mussel *Photo by Dave Brenner Michigan Sea Grant*

Todd White scrapes mussels off the bow of the *Michigan* *Photo by Robert Underhill*

41

Artifacts

Hidden below deck, the dishes that the crew ate from are still neatly stacked in wooden racks in the galley. The bell that Captain Prindiville used to summon the crew is below deck. The engine is in such good shape, it appears that, with a little grease, it could run again.

The most impressive and moving sight on the shipwreck is deep within the stern of the sunken steamer in a small cabin that was used as a workroom. Inside, stowed neatly on a shelf and upon the workbench are seven brass oil lanterns. They were likely put there by George Sheldon before abandoning the ship. These were the same lanterns that George kept lit and which helped guide *Arctic* towards the trapped ship.

42

The ship's bell below deck *Photo by Todd White*

The anchors at the bow *Photo by Robert Underhill*

The ships' wheel *Photo by Robert Underhill*

Brass lanterns on the shelf and workbench in a workroom near the stern   *Photo by Robert Underhill*

43

A True Story

ICEBOUND! is based on a true story that was developed from newspaper accounts about the struggles of the captain and crew of SS *Michigan* while they were trapped in the ice off western Michigan for 43 days in 1885. George Sheldon was the porter aboard the ship and the story of his heroic deeds was told by reporters. George's family story, the dialogue and details of the day-to-day activities have been created because the newspapers did not report that level of detail.

Captain Redmond Prindiville lived to be 87 years old and was laid to rest in Chicago's Calvary Cemetery, marked by an unusual family monument: a large boulder.

44

Prindiville family grave *Photo by Robert Gadbois*

Ross Richardson visits George Sheldon's grave in Grand Haven, Michigan *Photo by author*

George Sheldon was promoted to Second Engineer and served aboard the carferry *City of Milwaukee*. Sadly, however, due to illness which stemmed from his exposure while icebound on Lake Michigan, he died only five years after SS *Michigan* sank. He was buried in Forest Home Cemetery in Grand Haven, MI.

In Memory of a True Hero
George Sheldon 1863 - 1890

Glossary

Compass Directions

North: *0 degrees*

South: *180 degrees*

East: *90 degrees*

West: *270 degrees*

Northwest: *315 degrees*

Southwest: *225 degrees*

Crew member Ranks

Captain: *The chief officer who has authority over others.*

First Mate: *The officer of a vessel next in command beneath the captain.*

Engineer: *The officer in charge of the running of the engine.*

Clerk: *The crewman responsible for record keeping.*

Steward: *The person who waits on and is responsible for the comfort of ship's passengers.*

Cook: *Often the most well-respected man on board since he prepared the meals.*

Porter: *Crewman responsible for carrying luggage and supplies.*

General Terms used in ICEBOUND!

Icebound: *Held fast or hemmed in by ice.*

Pack Ice: *Floating ice packed together.*

Rations: *A fixed portion of food allotted in times of scarcity.*

Scuttled: *The purposeful sinking of a vessel.*

Nautical Terms

Aye, Aye: *Another way to say "Yes, Sir."*

Capstan: *A mechanical device used to haul up an anchor or to tighten docking lines in port.*

Steamship: *A ship, sometimes called a steamer, in which the primary method of propulsion is steam power, typically driving a propeller or paddlewheel. The SS Michigan was propeller-driven. SS is an abbreviation for steamship.*

Bow: *The forward end of a vessel.*

Stern: *The after end of a vessel.*

Port: *The left-hand side of a vessel, facing forward.*

Starboard: *The right-hand side of a vessel, facing forward.*

Aft: *At, close to, or toward the stern.*

Wheelhouse: *An enclosed area, usually on the bridge of a vessel, from which the vessel is controlled when under way.*

Davits: *Any of various types of small cranes that project over the side of a ship and are used to hoist boats, anchors, and cargo.*

Porthole: *A hinged, watertight window in the side of a vessel, round or with rounded corners, for admitting air and light.*

Knots: *A unit of speed used in water-based navigation.*

Icebound!

The Adventures of Young George Sheldon and the SS *Michigan*

First published in hard cover edition in Michigan, USA in 2008
In-Depth Editions
www.in-deptheditions.com

Printed and bound in China

Library of Congress Control Number: 2007941673

ISBN: 978-0-9801750-1-1

ICEBOUND!

The Adventures of Young George Sheldon and the *SS Michigan*

This book is dedicated to Cella and Taya.
Although they are too young to appreciate my fascination with shipwrecks and history, my daughters were the inspiration for this book. I am grateful for my husband, Jack, who shares my passion for diving and preserving maritime history and who helped lead our team to the wreck of the SS *Michigan*. I would like to thank Ross Richardson for his painstaking collection and transcription of newspaper articles, Craig Rich for his research in dramatizing the story, David Trotter for his talent in finding shipwrecks, and Joan Forsberg for her editing and introduction to the world of publishing. Lastly, without Elizabeth Trembley's encouragement, mentoring, and friendship, this book would not have been possible.
-*Valerie van Heest*

ABOUT THE AUTHOR/ILLUSTRATOR

Director of Michigan Shipwreck Research Associates and a member of the Women Divers Hall of Fame, Valerie van Heest has explored and documented shipwrecks for over 20 years. She is a 2007 recipient of the Historical Society of Michigan award for excellence of achievement in the collection, preservation and promotion of State and local history. Valerie has written extensively for a variety of magazines and periodicals and has been a contributor to many books, newspaper articles, and museum exhibits. Her work has been featured in the books, *Voices of the Sweetwater Seas* by Bill Keefe and *Shipwreck Hunter* by Gerry Volgenau. Valerie has also written and directed more than a dozen documentary films. She is a regular presenter at museums, libraries, and film festivals, sharing the dramatic stories of ships gone missing on the Great Lakes and has appeared on television news networks as well as on the Discovery Channel. Valerie spearheads MSRA's search for ships lost off western Michigan which has resulted in the discovery of many new shipwrecks.

Combining her interest in maritime history with the skills she developed in over twenty-five years in the field of architectural and graphic design, Valerie created the unique illustrations featured in this book and designed the book's layout.